Vol 12

MAZE

FOR KIDS

Ages 4-6

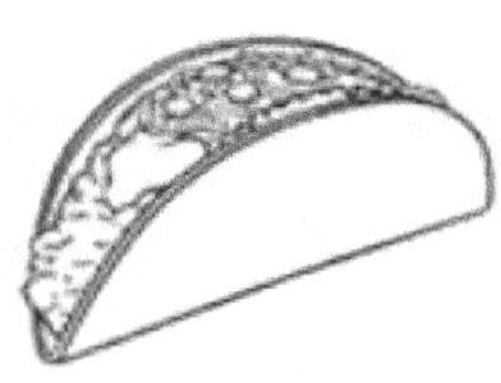
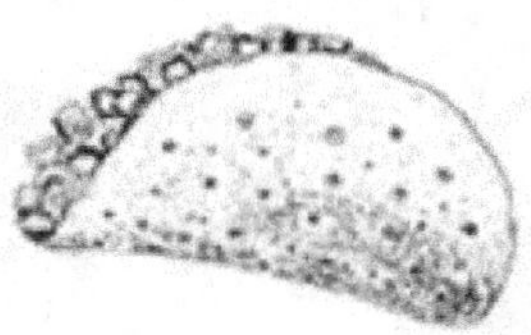

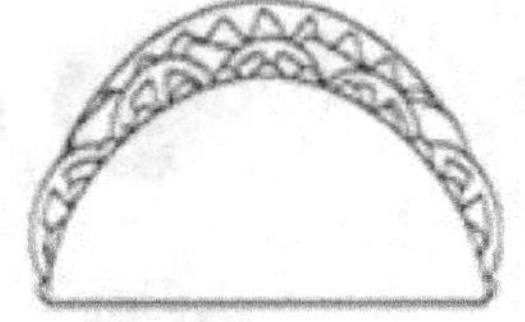
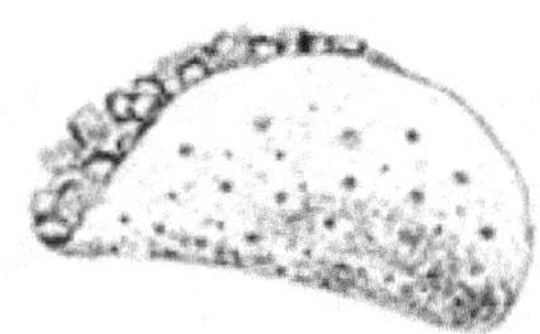

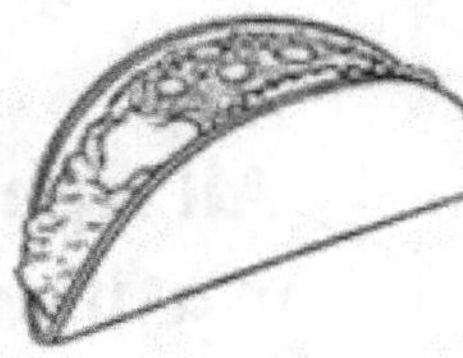

MAZE BOOK

SOCIAL MEDIA

(f) /MySweetBooks1

(t) /MySweetBooks1

(ig) /MySweetBooks1

(p) /MySweetBooks

Email Us : mysweetbooks1@gmail.com

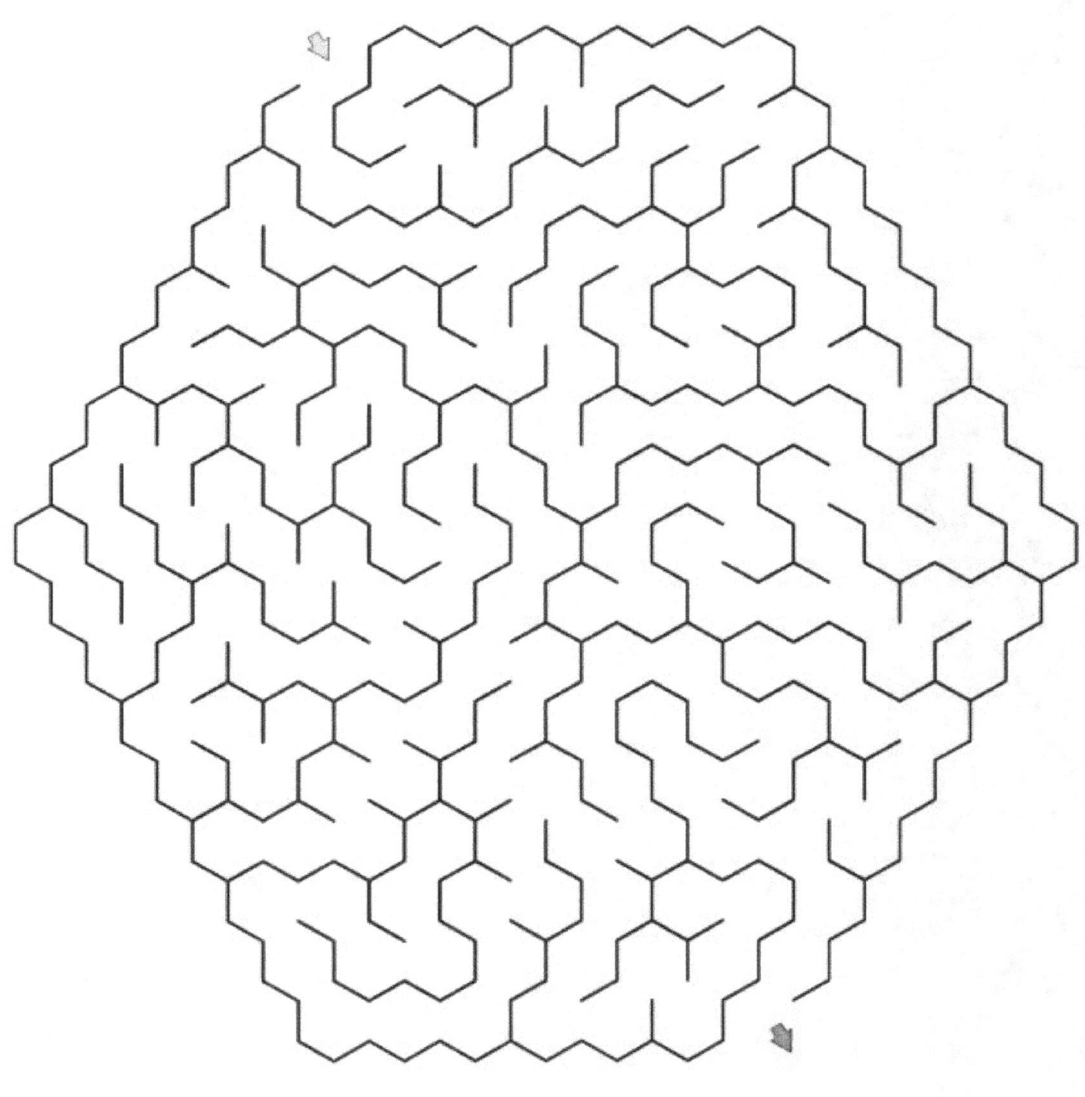

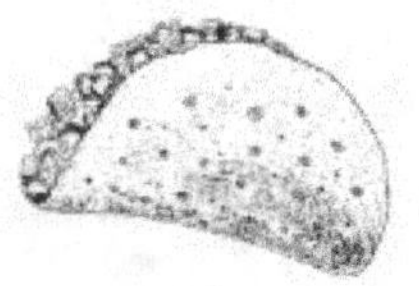

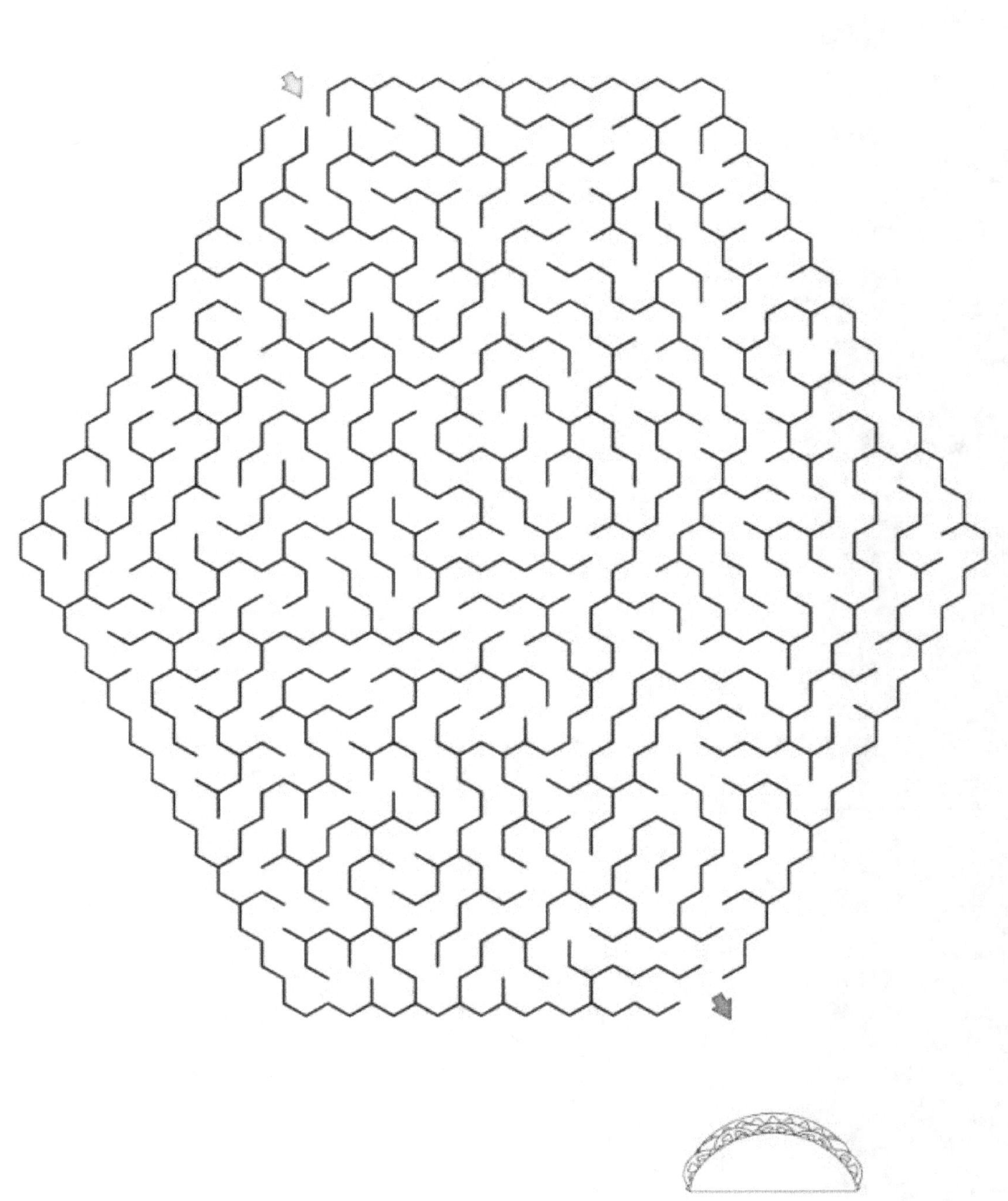

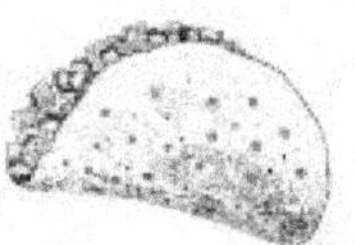

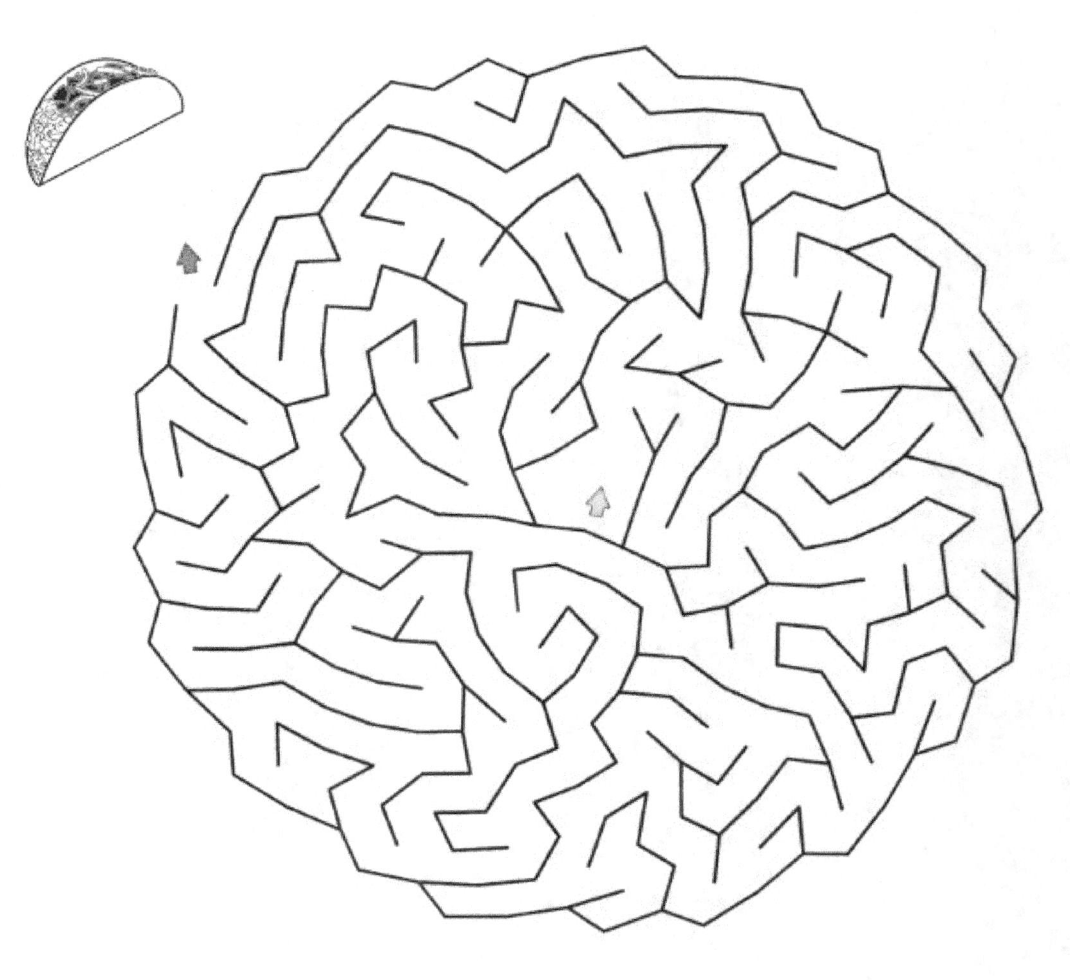

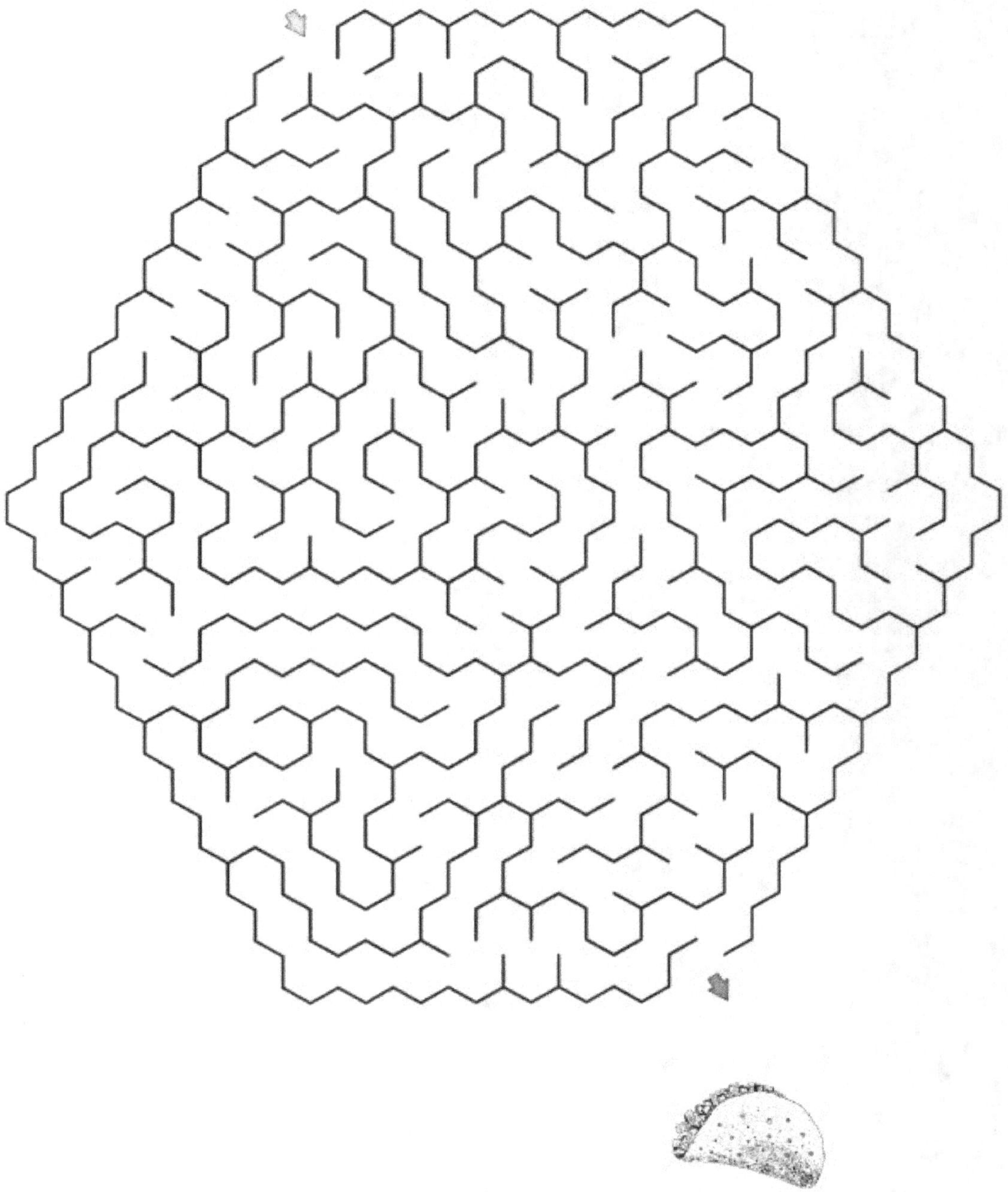

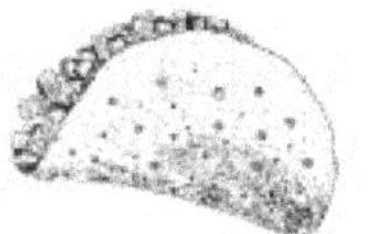

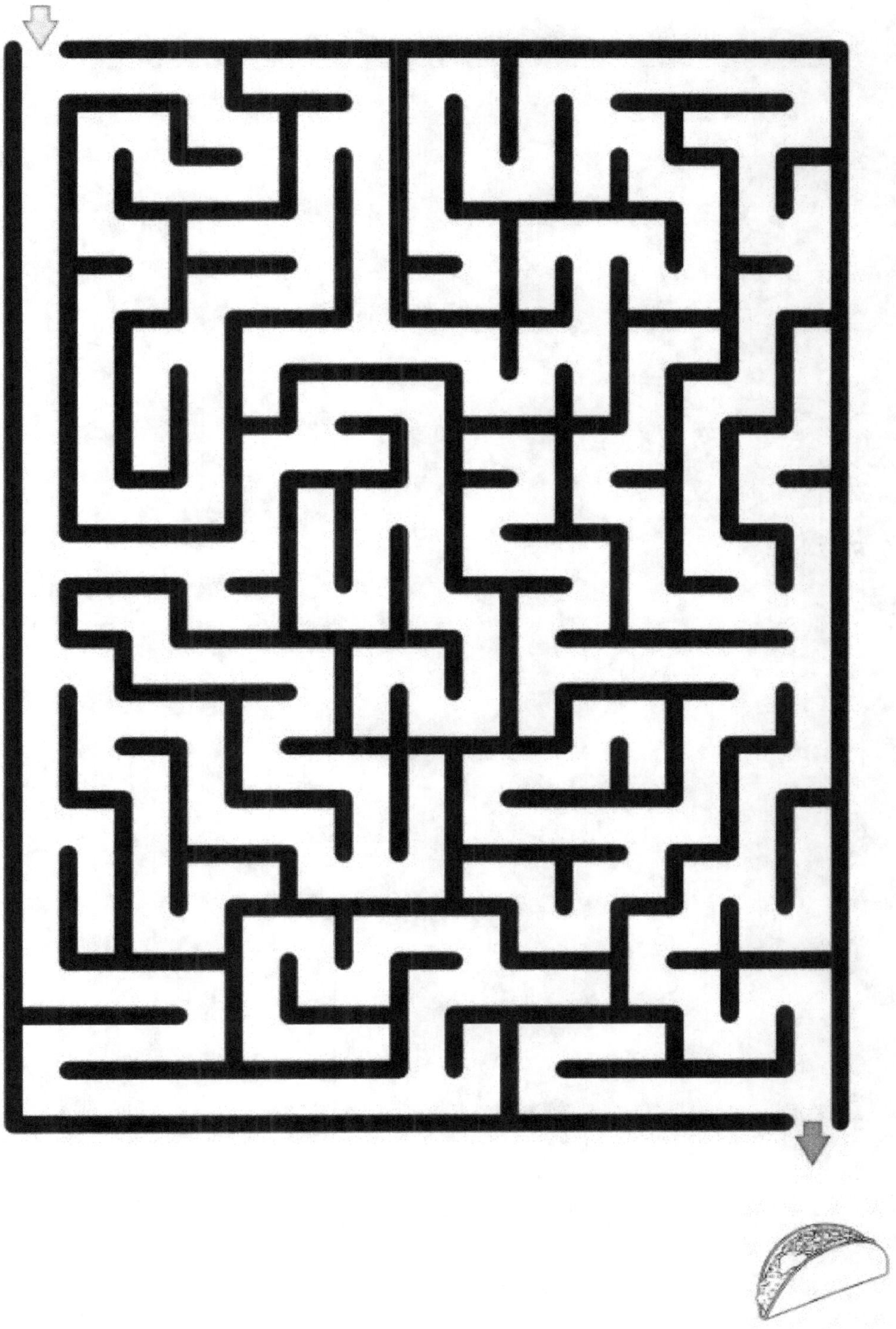

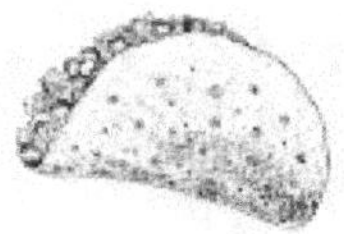

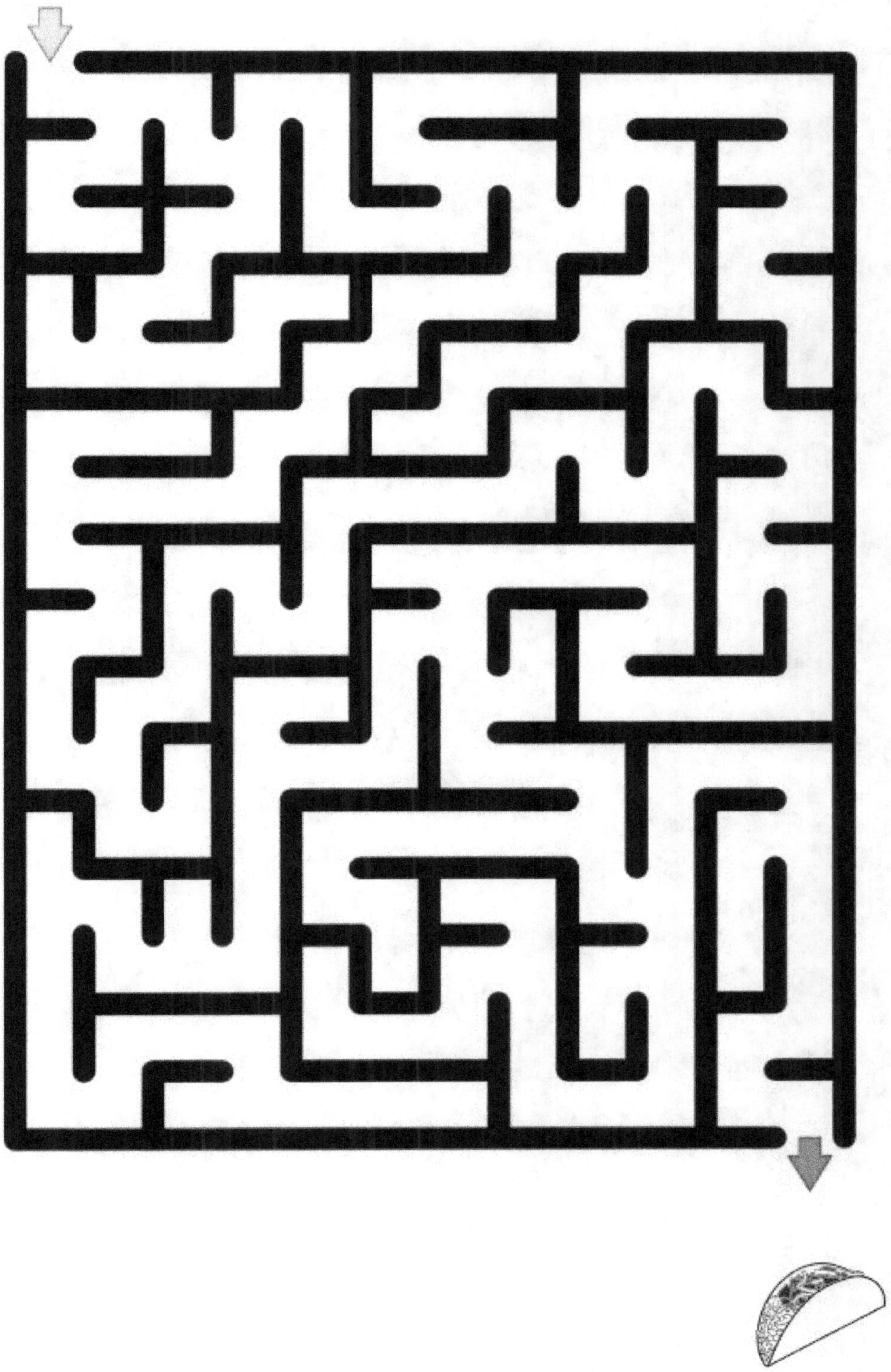

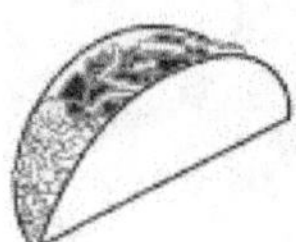

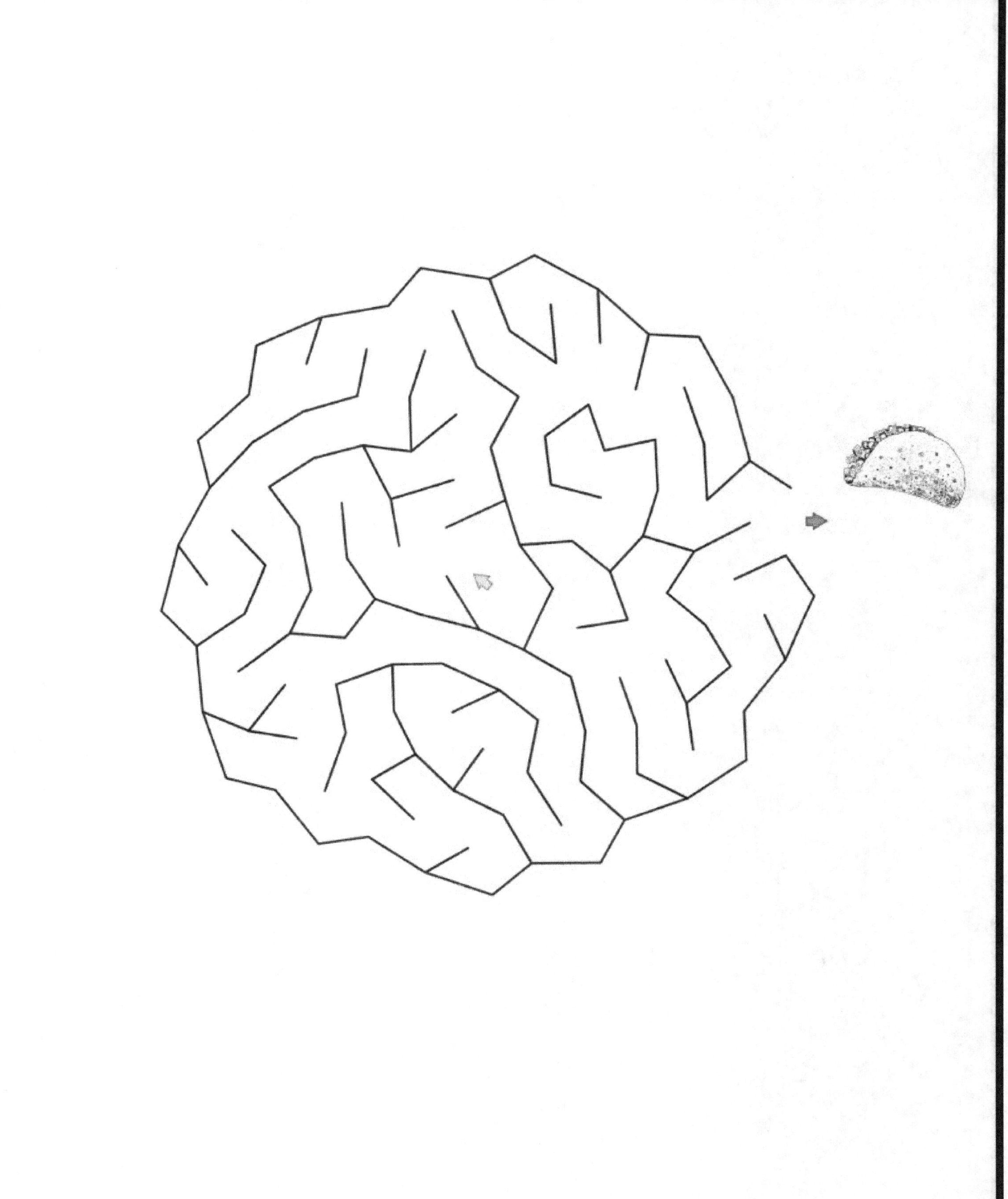

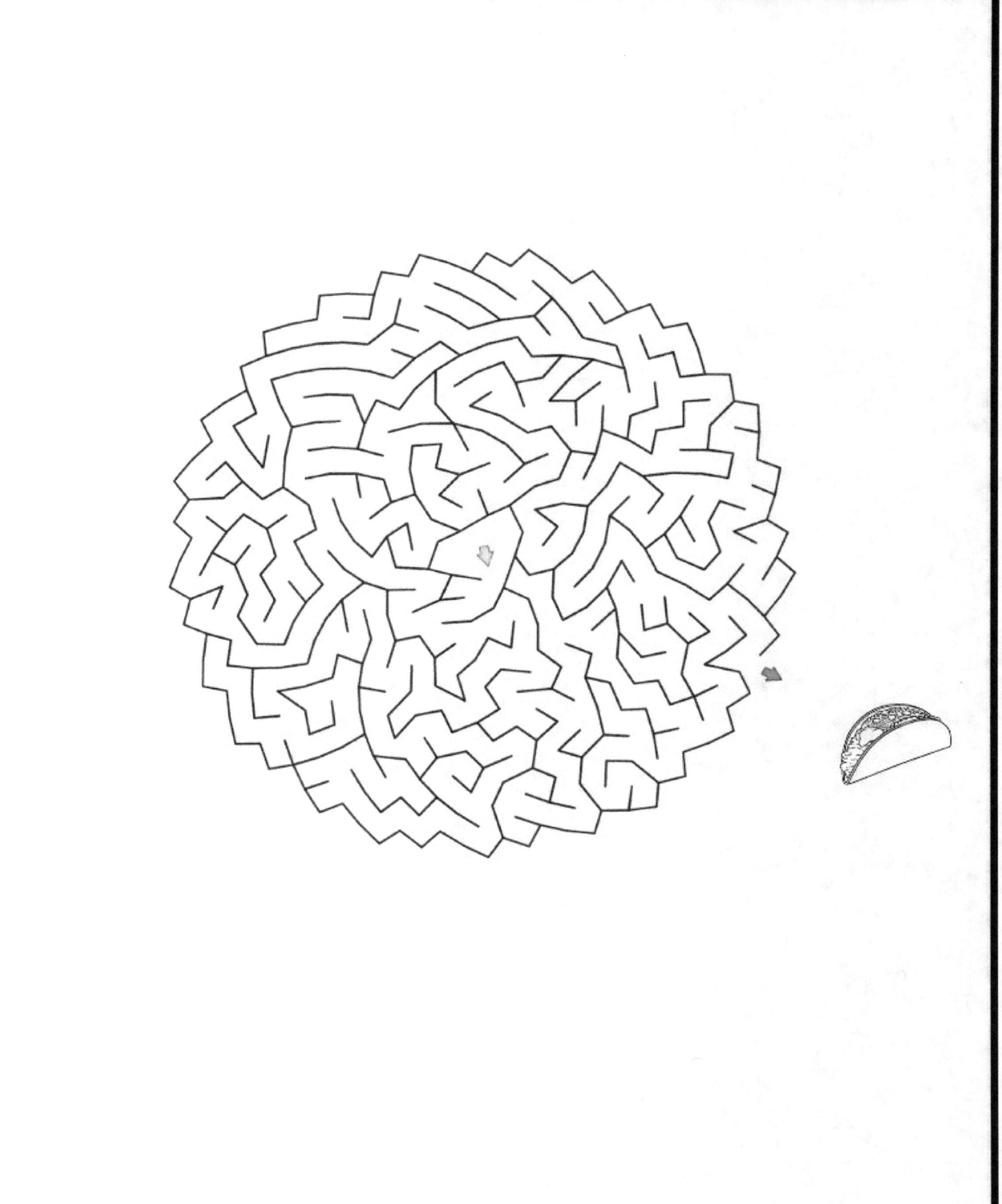

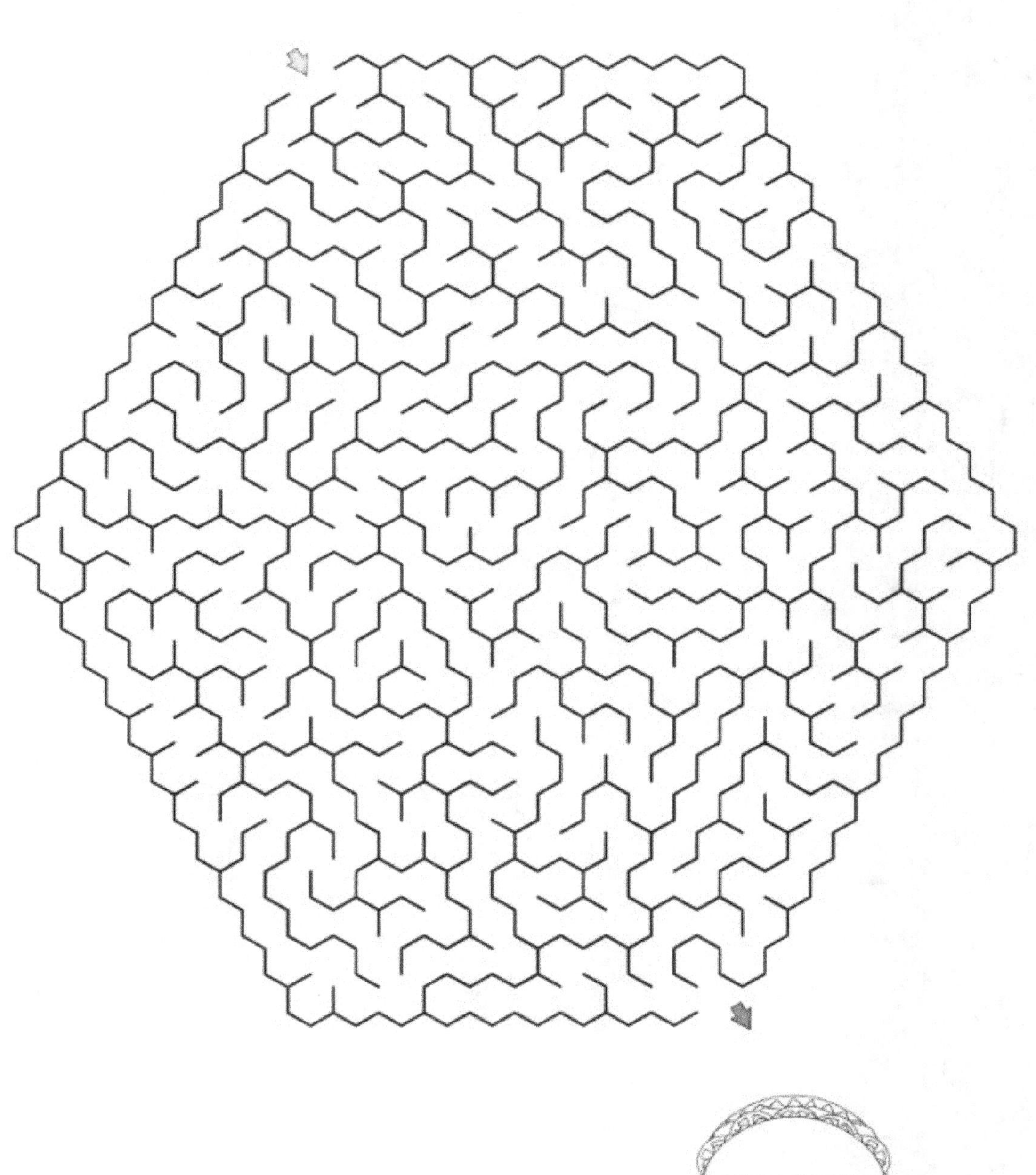

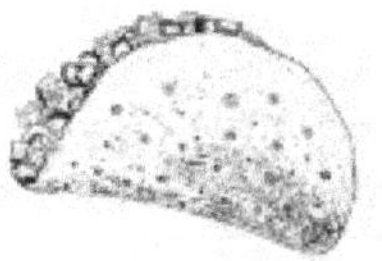

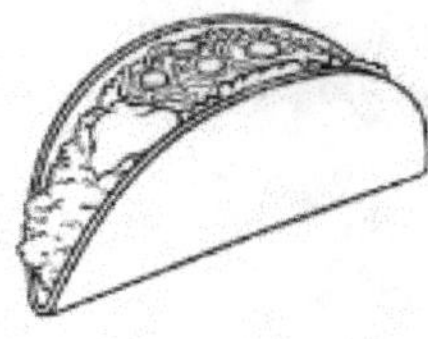

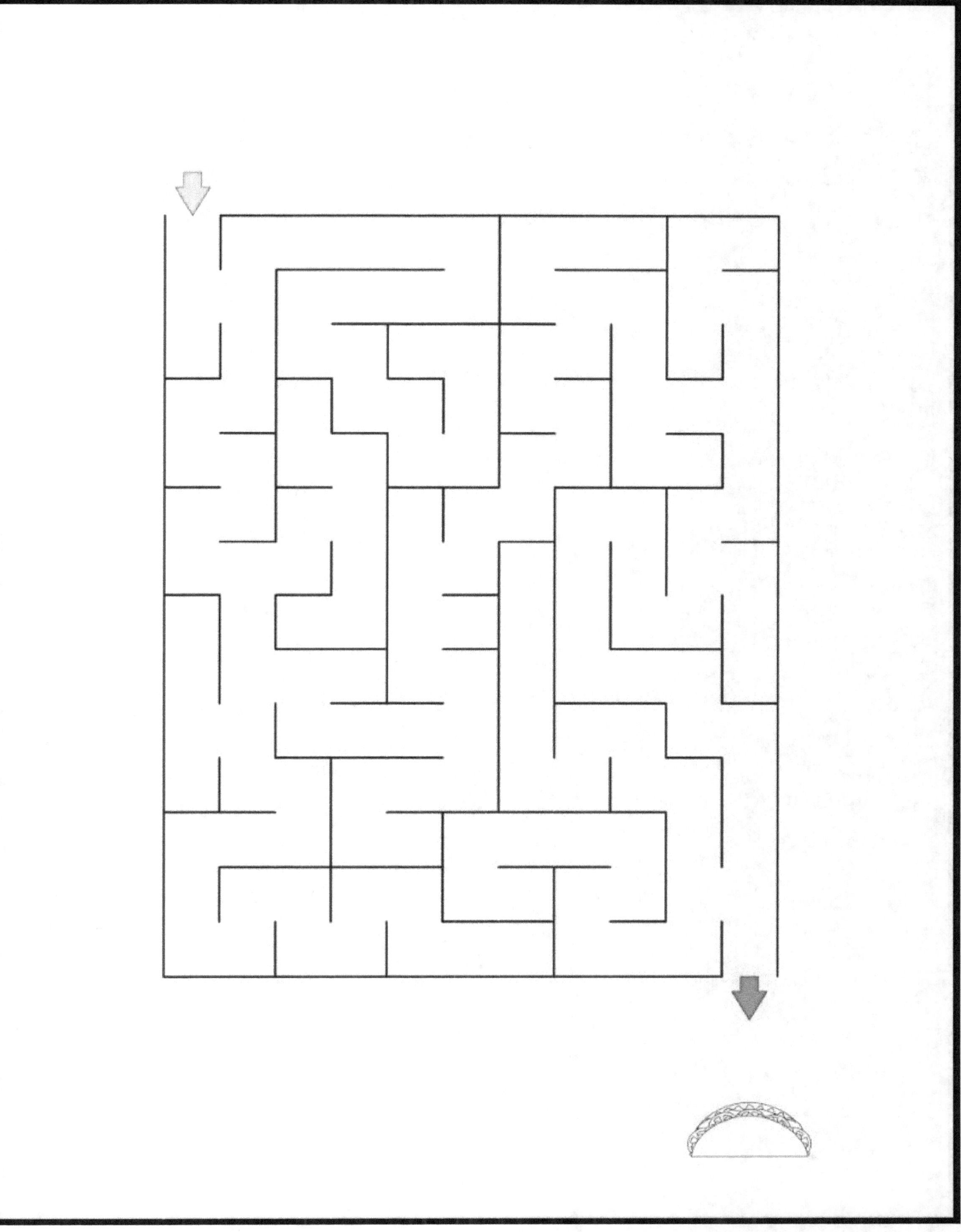

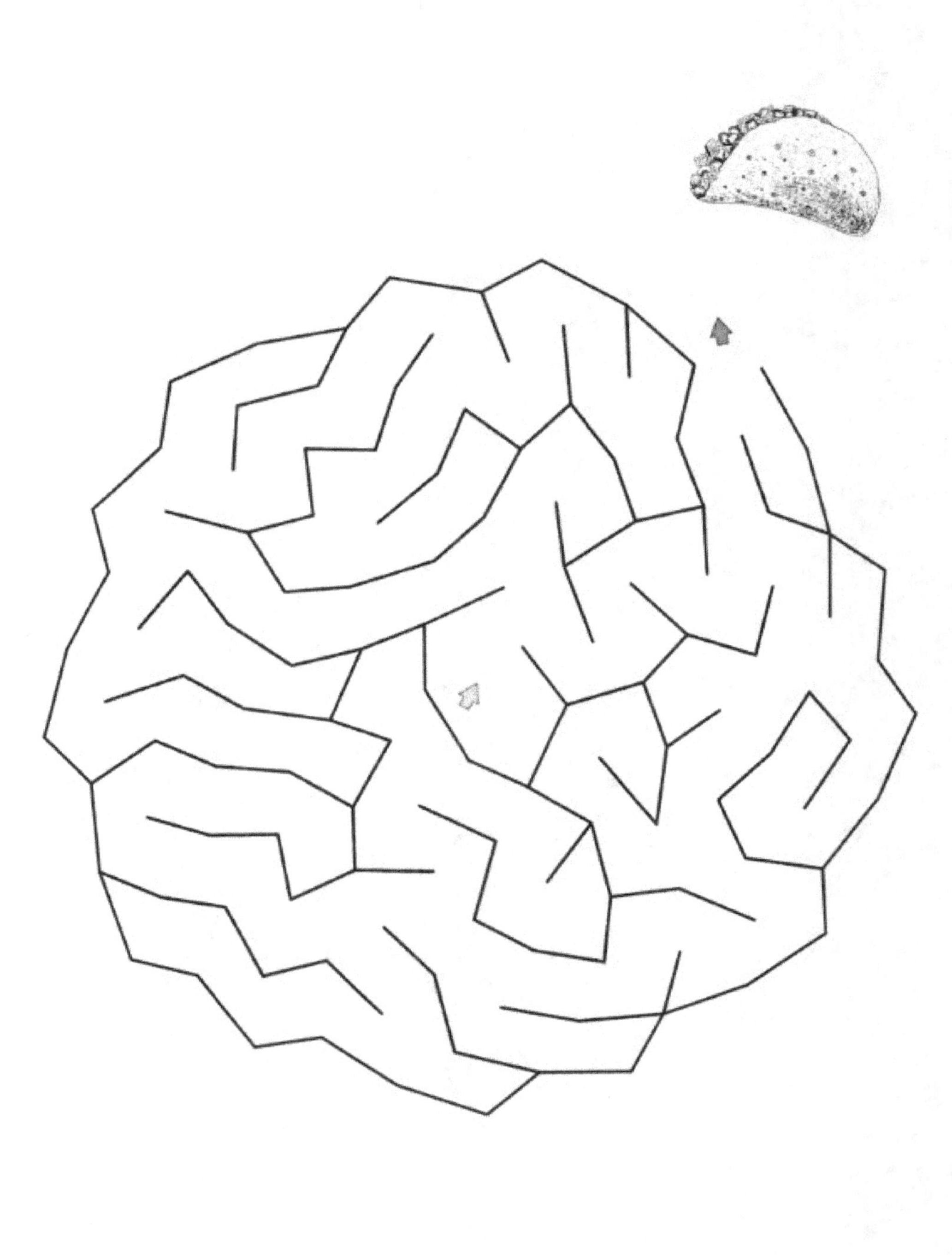

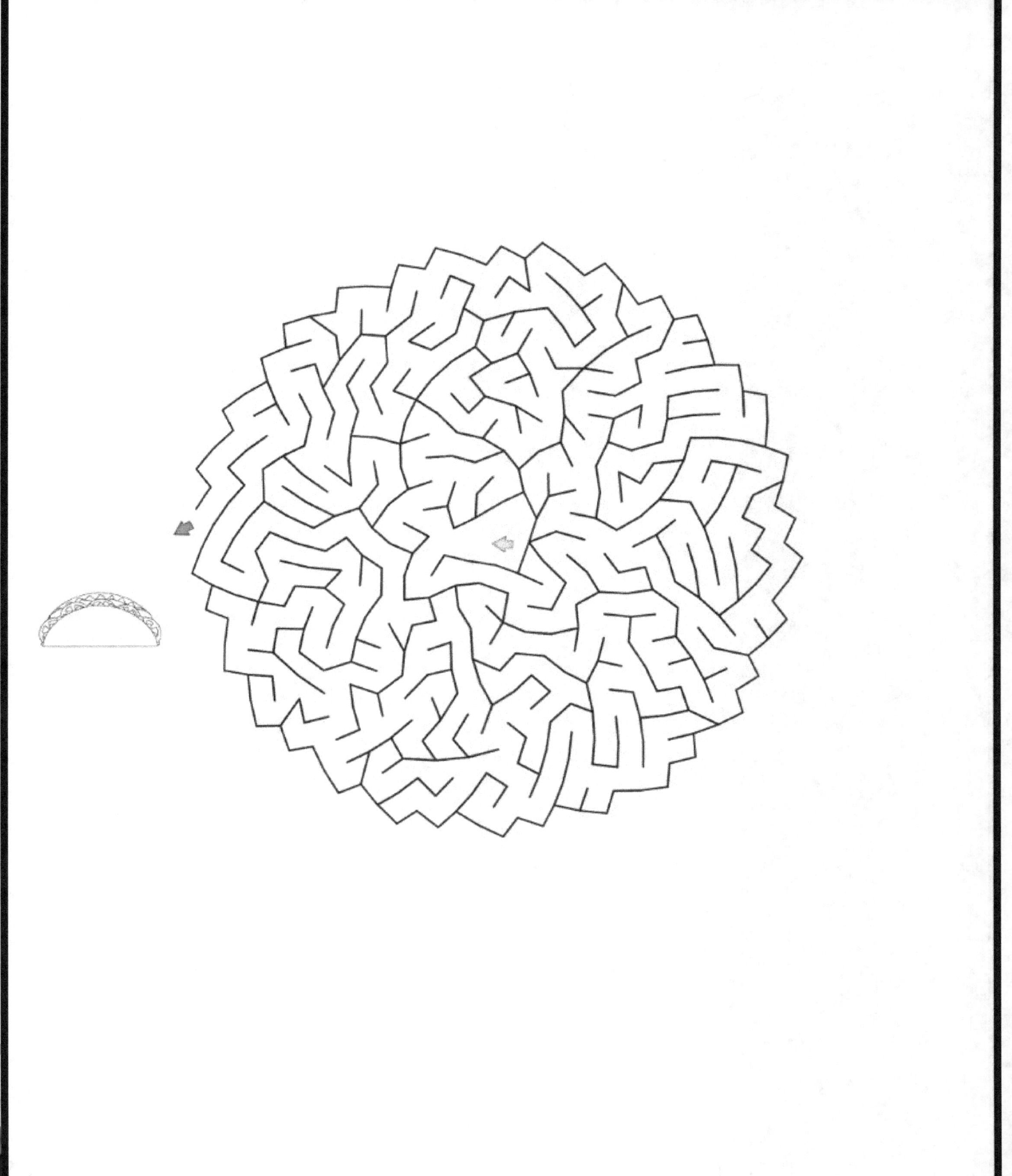

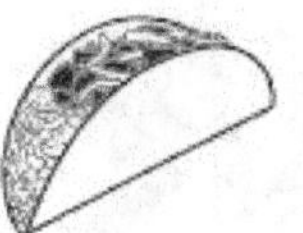

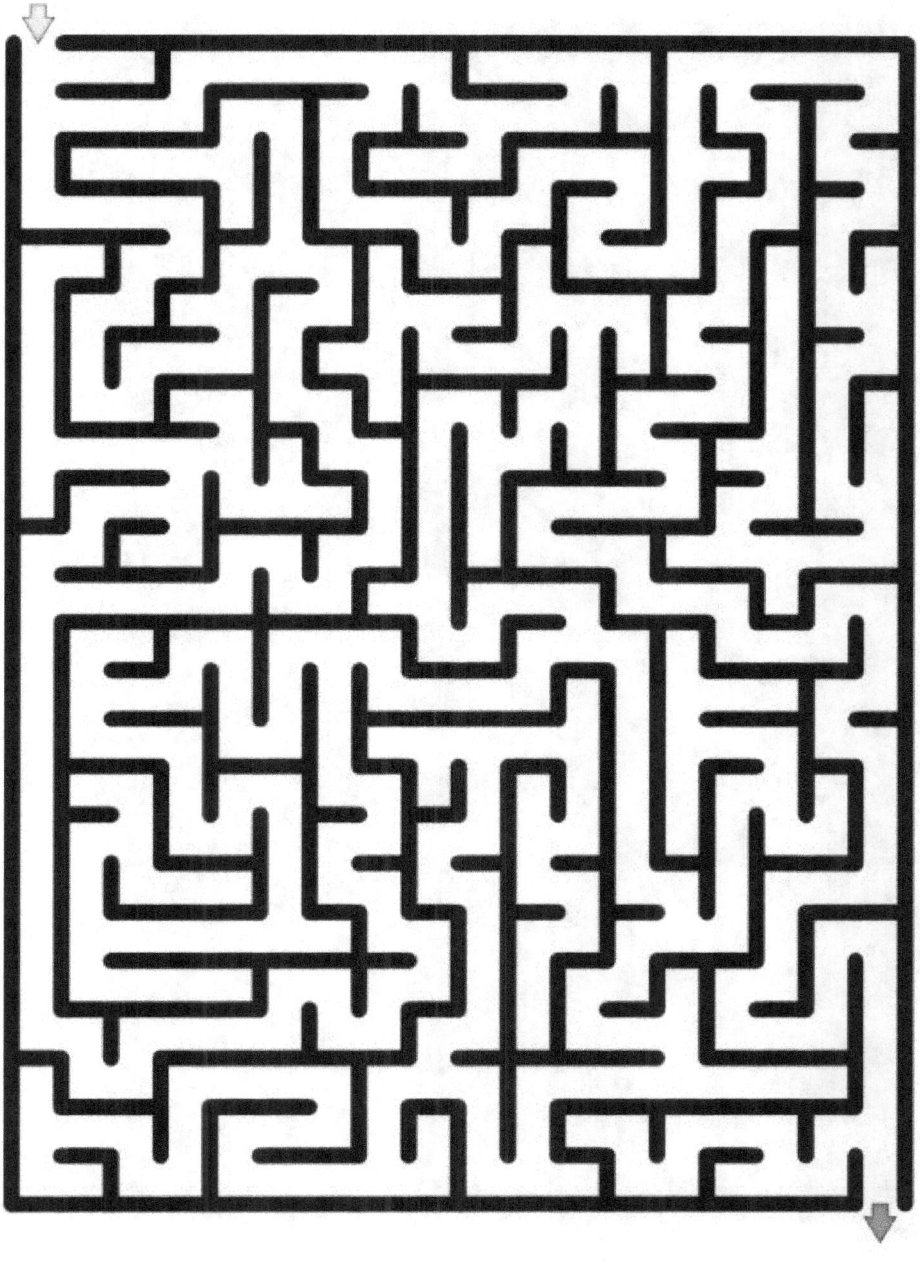

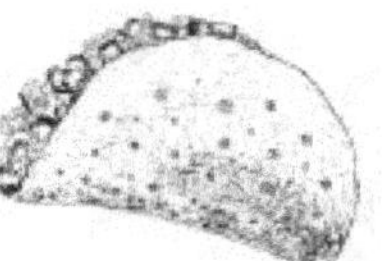

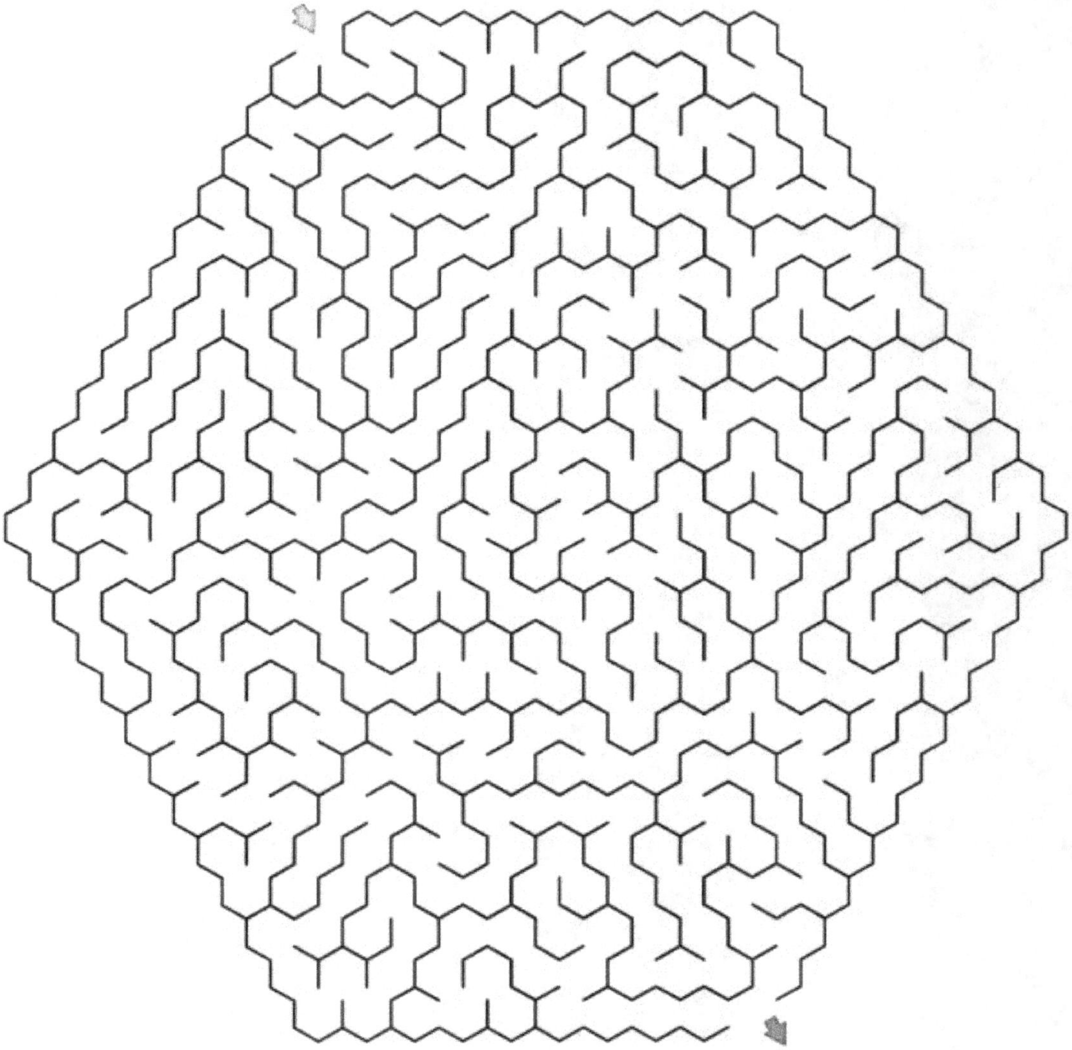

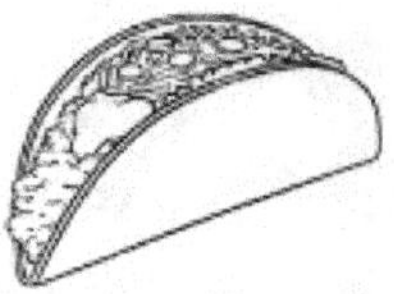